AF351628

Presented in partnership with the

1882
FOUNDATION

TICKET
Passenger Name:
Destination: SUMMIT TUNNEL
Date of Departure: 1866

Welcome aboard!

You're about to travel back in time to the snowy Sierra Nevada mountains of California, where thousands of brave workers chiseled, scraped, and blasted their way through the solid rock of the mountains to build a train tunnel for the Transcontinental Railroad.

Your expert historical guide? A man named **Wei Zhang** (pronounced "Way Jahng"). At the age of just 16, he helped to build a tunnel high in the Sierra Nevada mountains called Tunnel No. 6. Now it's commonly referred to as the **Summit Tunnel**. Wei is ready to share his journey with you—and trust us, it's a story you won't want to miss.

Get ready to color, learn, and imagine as we follow Wei's courageous path through mountains, snowstorms, and time. Many people don't know about the Chinese workers who made the Transcontinental Railroad possible. But we're here to change that because when we tell stories like Wei's, we help make sure everyone's hard work and courage is remembered...not just the people who made it into the history books.

Meet Young Wei

This is me, a long time ago. I was just 16 when I left my village in Guangdong, China. Life at home was really hard. There had been war, floods and droughts that destroyed farms, and many families, including mine, were hungry and poor. We couldn't find steady work, and some people were getting sick because they didn't have enough to eat.

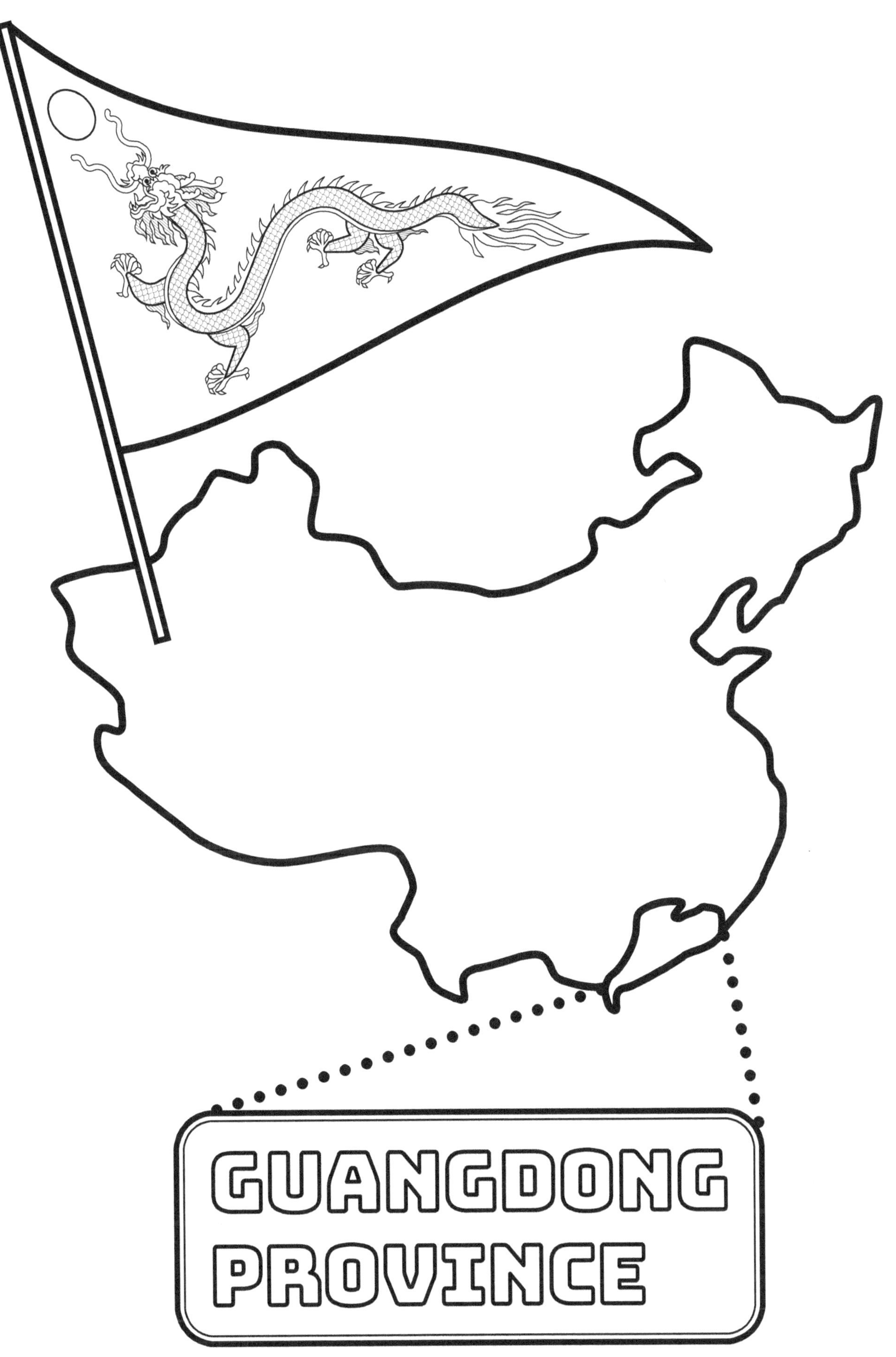

GUANGDONG
PROVINCE

So my uncle and I crossed the ocean to America, hoping we could find jobs and send money back to help our family survive.

We traveled more than 7,000 miles across the ocean, without knowing exactly what we'd find on the other side.

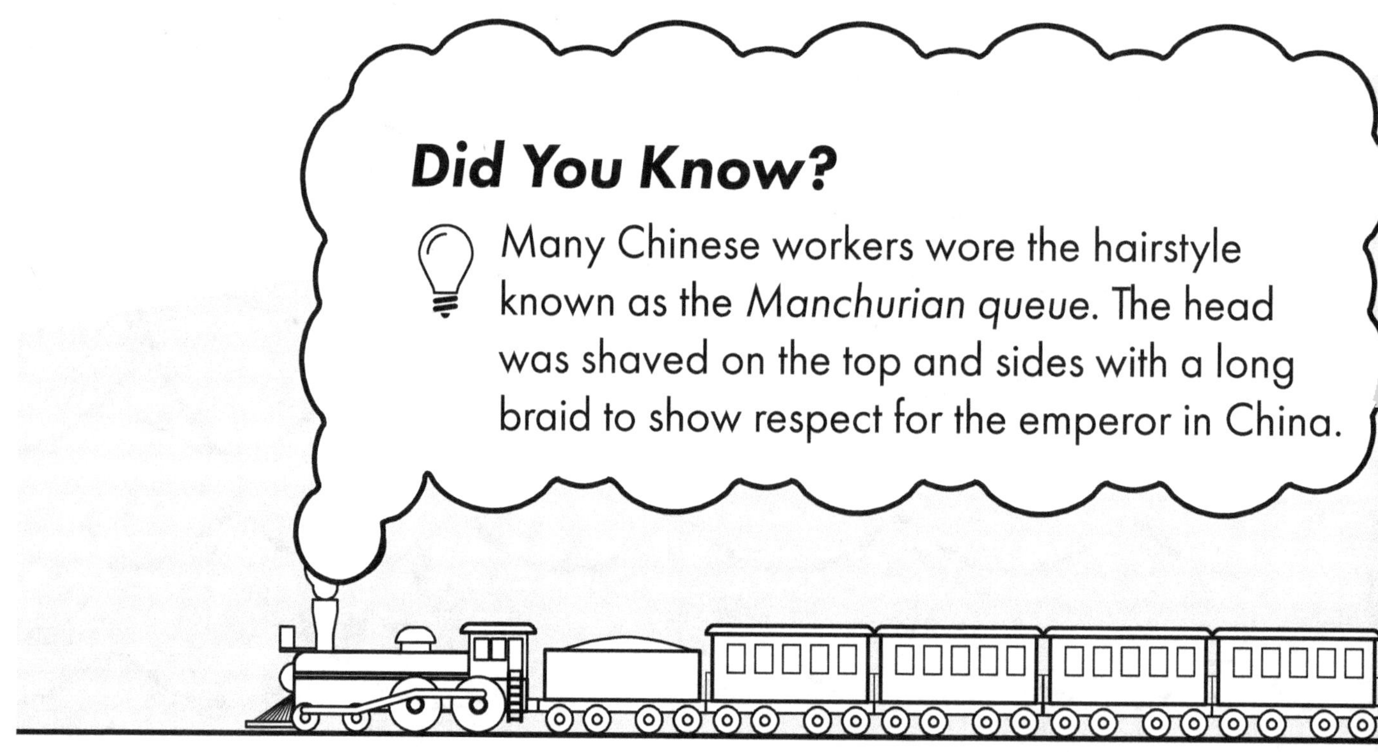

Did You Know?

Many Chinese workers wore the hairstyle known as the *Manchurian queue*. The head was shaved on the top and sides with a long braid to show respect for the emperor in China.

Arrival in America

But when we got to California, things weren't easy. The jobs were dangerous, and Chinese laborers were paid less than white workers, even when we did the same or harder work.

Many of us had come to America after hearing stories of a place called 'Gold Mountain'—a land where people said you could get rich just by working hard. But those promises weren't true.

Instead of gold, we found unfair treatment and unsafe jobs.

Still, we didn't have much choice. If we didn't stay and work, our families back home might not survive. And we couldn't afford to return to China empty handed.

So, we stayed.

We supported each other. We worked together. And we helped build something big...something no one thought we could do...

Wei's Big Move

Activity Page

- Use the **map artwork** on the following page showing Wei's personal route from Guangdong in China to San Francisco and up north into the Sierra Nevada.

- Focus on Wei's experience—not the entire railroad.

Activity Prompt

Follow Wei's journey! Use a pencil or crayon to trace his path across the ocean to California. Can you circle where you think Tunnel No. 6 might be in the Sierra Nevada?

Wei's Big Move

Bonus Challenge

 When Wei boarded the ship to California, he had no idea what it would be like. He couldn't look up where he was going on a computer or see pictures ahead of time. He had never even seen a map of where he was going. He just knew he had to go, to try and help his family survive.

How do you think Wei felt at that moment?

- Draw a picture of his face or write a word that describes what he might have been feeling.

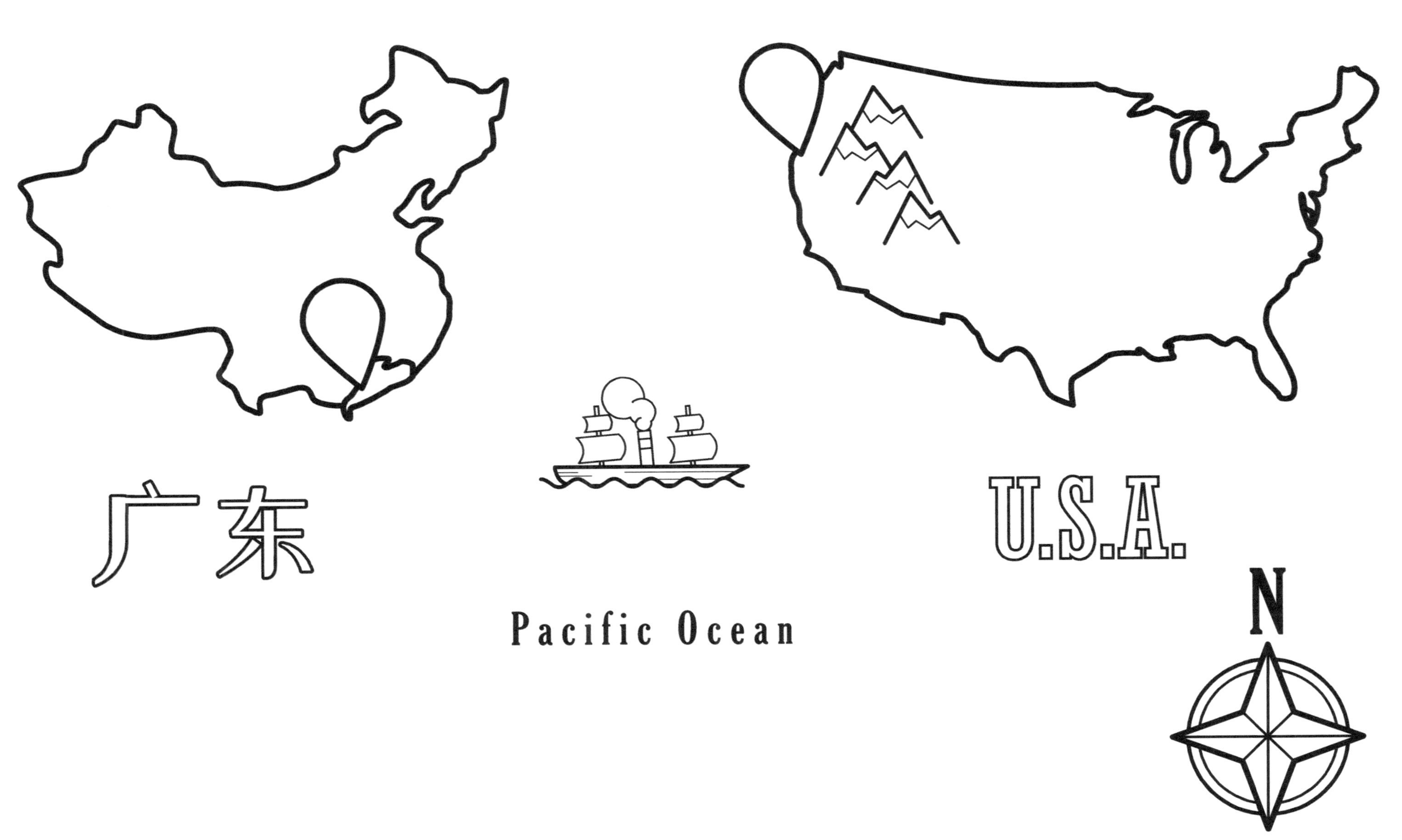

广东
U.S.A.
Pacific Ocean
N

A New Land

When we arrived in California, everything felt different—the food, the weather, even the sounds! We made our way into the Sierra Nevada mountains. That's where the Central Pacific Railroad had run into a huge problem: the mountains were too steep and rocky to build train tracks over. **They had to find a way through.**

But how do you dig through solid granite rock, high in the mountains, in freezing weather, with almost no machines?

That's when they turned to us.

Meeting in the Middle

The **Central Pacific Railroad** was the company building the train tracks across California. It was part of the Transcontinental Railroad, a massive train line that connected the East and West Coasts of the United States for the very first time. Before it was built, crossing the country took months by wagon, horseback, or even by sailing all the way around South America. The construction of the Transcontinental Railroad reduced travel time from the East coast to the West coast to only 10 days. The Central Pacific Railroad started building from California and headed east.

The other railroad company was called the **Union Pacific Railroad**—they started in the east and headed west. They planned to meet in the middle, in Promontory, Utah.

Promontory
UTAH

Follow the Tracks: Mapping the Transcontinental Railroad

Activity Prompt:

Use two different pencil or crayon colors to trace the two parts of the Transcontinental Railroad on the following page:

- Use one color to trace the **Central Pacific Railroad** (starting in California)

- Use another color to trace the **Union Pacific Railroad** (starting in Iowa)

They meet in **Promontory, Utah**. Can you find it on the map and draw a railroad spike there? A railroad spike is a long metal nail that helps hold train tracks in place.

Bonus Challenge:

Circle where you think **Tunnel No. 6 (Summit Tunnel)** might be in the Sierra Nevada mountains. That's where Wei and thousands of other Chinese workers helped build the most difficult part of the railroad.

Think About It:

The railroad helped connect people across the country, but what stories do maps sometimes leave out?

____

____

____

____

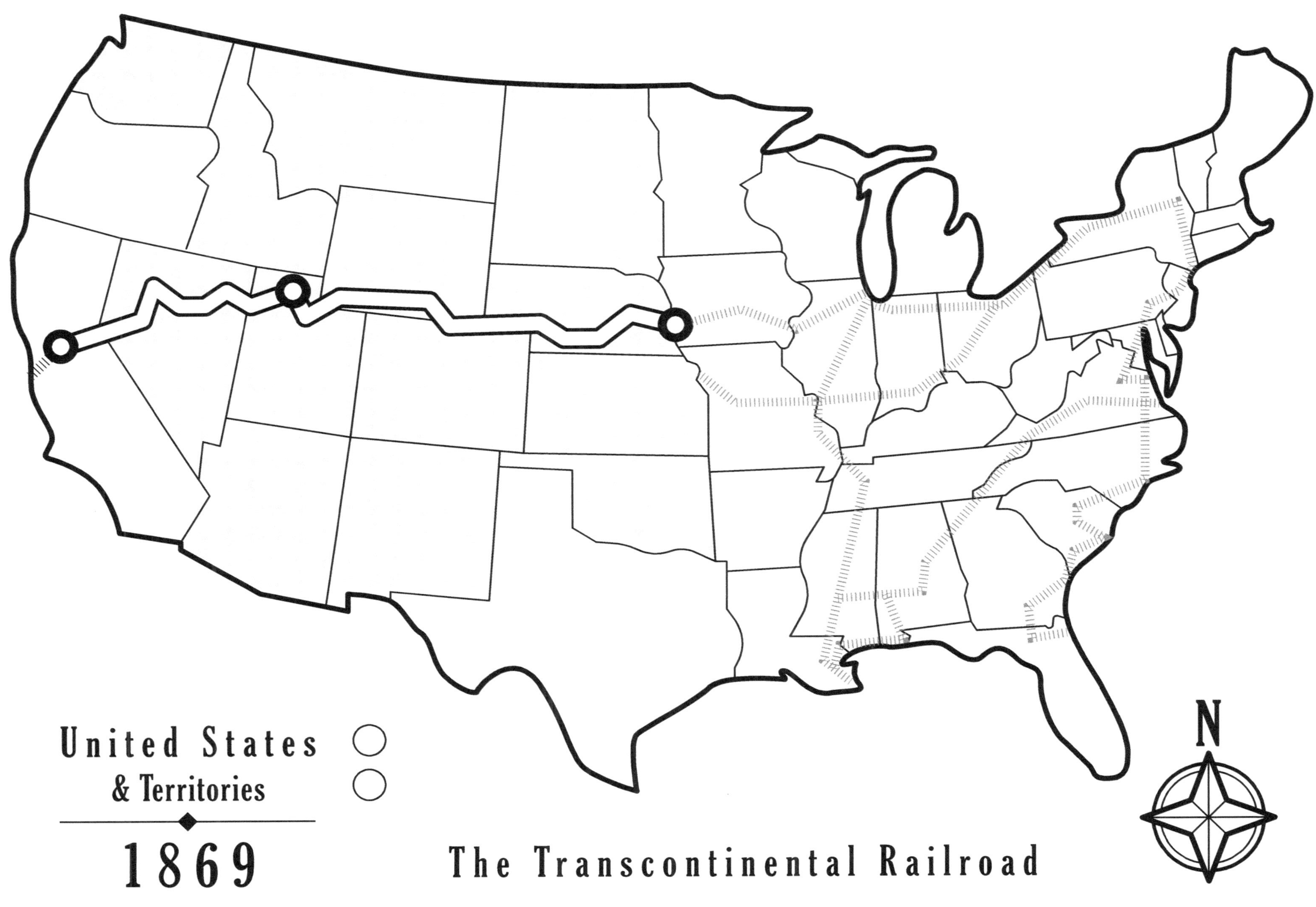

United States
& Territories
1869
The Transcontinental Railroad
N

Digging In

Building the train tunnel was incredibly dangerous. The mountain was made of solid granite rock, and winters were brutal: snowstorms, ice, and freezing winds. Many workers had already quit—mostly white Americans and European immigrants—because the conditions were just too hard.

But we stayed.

We needed the work. Our families back in China were counting on us to send money home. We didn't have savings or other options. And even though the pay was unfair, this was still one of the only jobs we were allowed to do.

So we kept going. We had to.

DONNER
SUMMIT
35ft
34ft
33ft

That's when the railroad company started recruiting more Chinese laborers. Some, like me, were hired from San Francisco. Others were already working in other parts of California or had been recruited through people they knew or word of mouth. Many of us were young adults, even teenagers, working to support our families back home.

We were sent to build a tunnel called Tunnel No. 6.

It was cold. It was dark. It was dangerous.

To break through the granite rock, we used black powder and nitroglycerin—explosives that could be deadly if handled wrong. First, we carved holes into the stone by hand. Then we packed the powder in holes, lit a fuse...and ran. Fast. You had to hope you got far enough away before it blew.

TUNNEL
No. 6
19ft
14ft
9ft

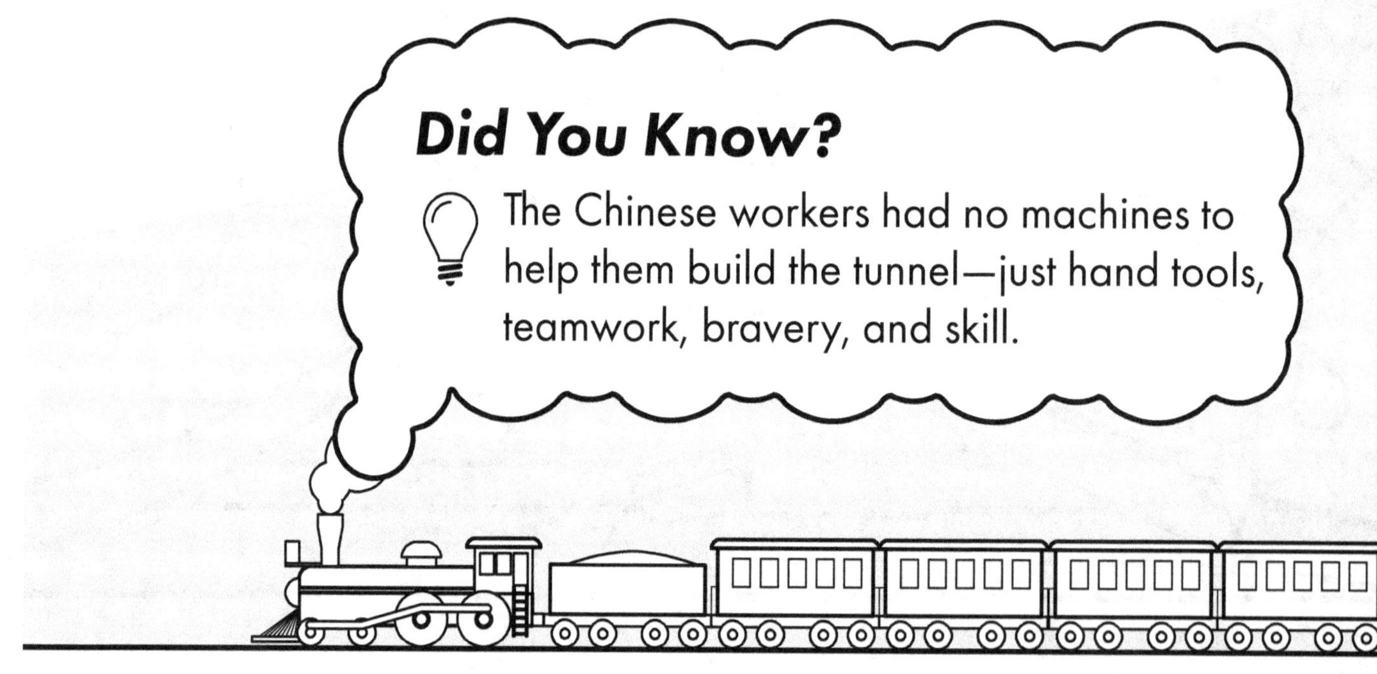

Did You Know?

The Chinese workers had no machines to help them build the tunnel—just hand tools, teamwork, bravery, and skill.

Where is Tunnel No. 6?

Location:

Donner Summit is where Tunnel No. 6 was built—in the snowy Sierra Nevada mountains of California. It was the longest of the 15 tunnels the Chinese workers built through the Sierra Nevada mountains and one of the hardest to complete! It is 19 feet high, 16 feet wide, and 1,659 feet long.

Reflection Prompt:

What do you think Wei felt when he first saw the big mountain he had to blast a tunnel through? Write or draw your answer here.

Tunnel No. 6
Tunnel No. 7
Tunnel No. 8
DONNER PASS
SIERRA NEVADA
California

Blast by Blast

Once the hole was ready, we packed it with explosives. When the blast went off, it shattered the rock, but left behind sharp rubble, thick smoke, and dust that made it hard to breathe. We worked by lantern light. Sometimes, even candlelight.

Even a small mistake could mean injury...or worse. Sometimes, the blast didn't go off right away. Other times, just a bit of powder floating in the air could spark too soon. But we didn't give up.

We kept working.

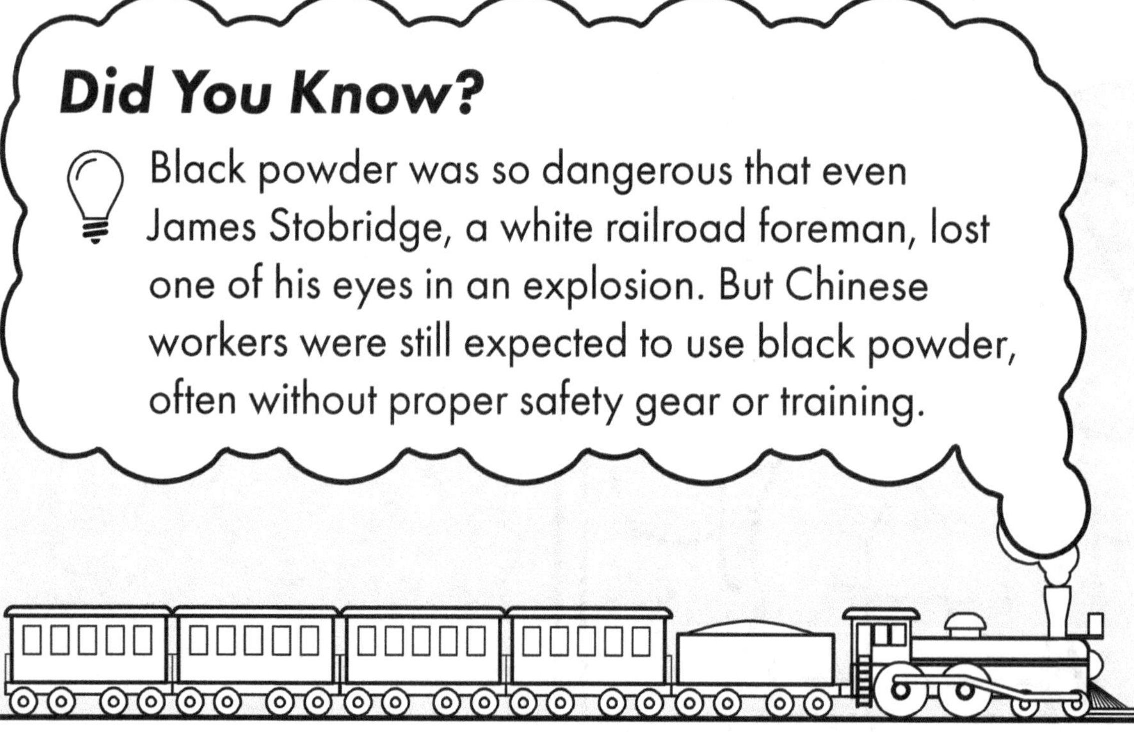

Tools of the Tunnel

Activity Prompt:

Circle the tools that the Chinese laborers actually used to dig through the mountain in 1866 to build the Summit Tunnel. Can you name them all? (*Hint: You can check your answers using the answer key on Page 111. No cheating though!*)

All Seasons, All Hours

Our teams worked in shifts that never stopped. Some nights, we barely slept. Other times, we only had a few minutes to rest before heading back out to dig.

No matter how hard it got, we kept going.

The Land Wasn't Empty

Long before the railroad, many Native people lived across the land the trains would later cross.

The land wasn't empty. It was home.

As the railroad expanded west across the country, many Native communities, particularly in the Plains, were forced off their land.. Their homes were stolen, their communities were uprooted, and their way of life changed forever.

The railroad helped the country in many ways. It allowed goods to move faster, connected distant towns and cities, and helped some people find new jobs and homes.

But all of that came at a cost: while some people gained land, money, and power, many others, especially Native communities, lost their homes, their freedom, and their safety.

That's part of the story, too.

Reflection Prompt:

How do you think it felt for Native people to lose their homes to the railroad? What can we do to make sure we listen to and honor their stories today?

The Longest Winter

Chinese workers often camped near the tunnel in tents or makeshift shelters.

Protecting the Railroad

We also built long wooden sheds over the train tracks, so snow wouldn't block the rails.

**It was bitter cold.
But we kept going.**

Did You Know?

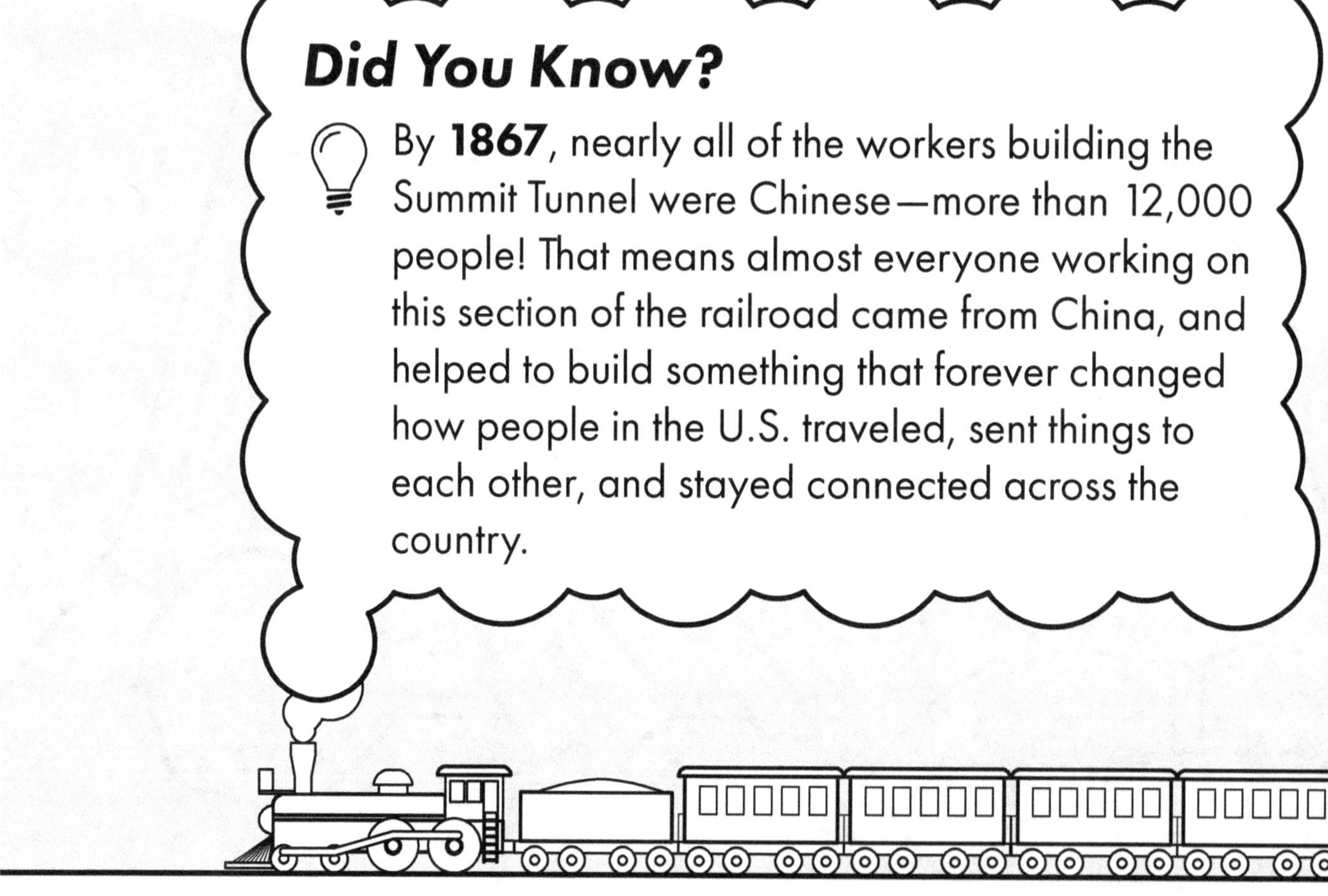

By **1867**, nearly all of the workers building the Summit Tunnel were Chinese—more than 12,000 people! That means almost everyone working on this section of the railroad came from China, and helped to build something that forever changed how people in the U.S. traveled, sent things to each other, and stayed connected across the country.

Snow Tunnel Maze!

Activity Prompt:

Wei and his crew had to dig tunnels through deep snow just to reach their work during long, freezing winters. Help them find their way from the camp to the worksite through the tunnel maze. Watch out for icy patches, lost tools, or broken lanterns along the way!

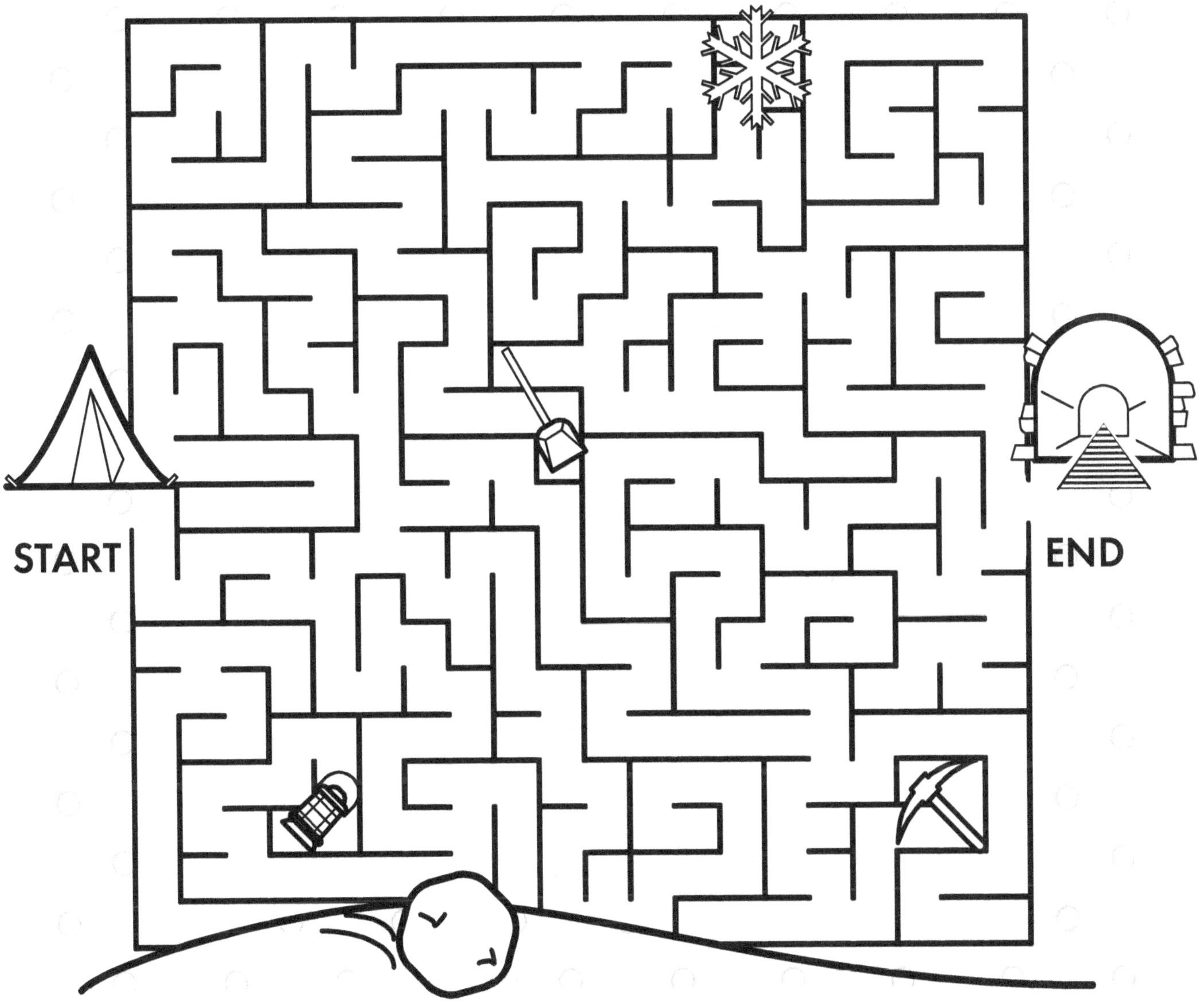

10 Miles in One Day!

Mile 10

The Summer We Spoke Up

Even though we worked the hardest, we weren't treated fairly. We got paid less for our work than white workers, and we were given the most dangerous jobs.

So in the summer of 1867, five thousand of us went on strike. We refused to keep working until we got fair pay and shorter hours. But the railroad company punished us. They stopped sending food and supplies to our camps.

After eight days with no food, we had no choice but to go back to work.

The railroad company never said yes to our demands, but a few months later, the pay for some workers went up. We don't know for sure if it was because of the strike.

But we do know this: we took action together. And that mattered.

Reflection Prompt:

 Have you ever spoken up or taken action when something that wasn't fair? What do you imagine it felt like for the workers to take action stand together and ask for change?

____

____

____

____

____

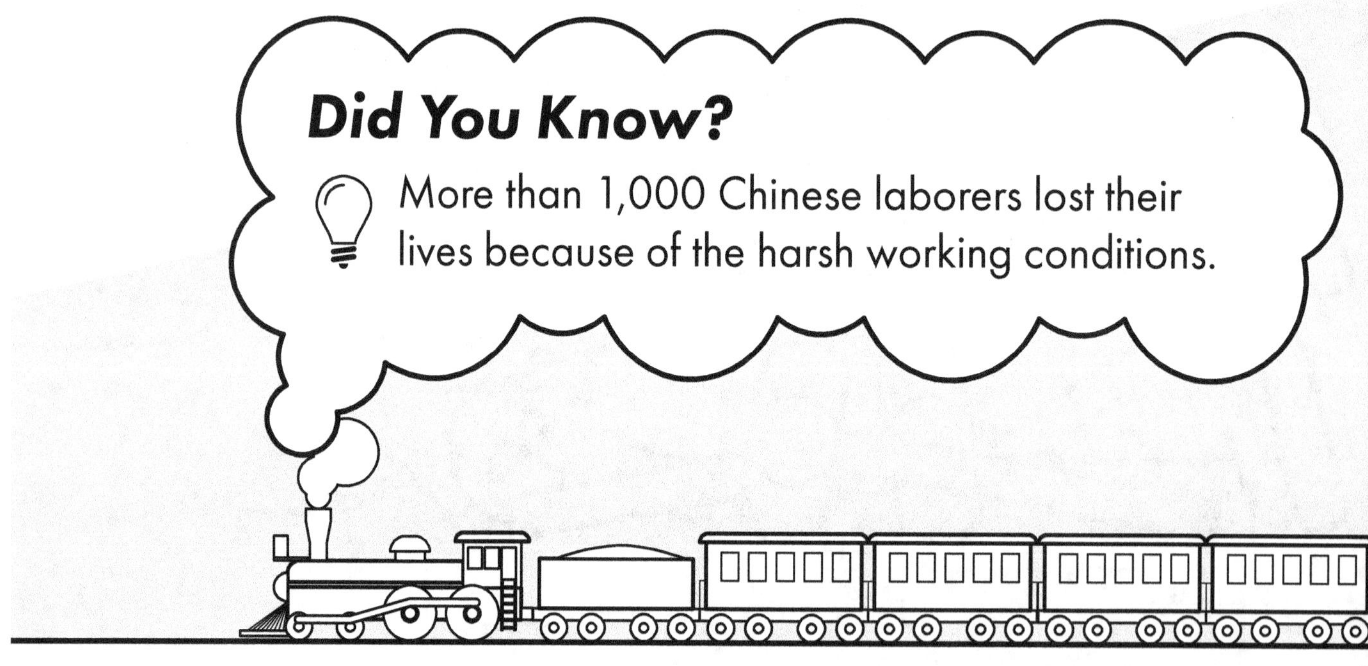

Did You Know?
More than 1,000 Chinese laborers lost their
lives because of the harsh working conditions.

Remembering the Ones We Lost

Our work was dangerous. We shared what little food we had. We helped dig each other out after avalanches. We kept each other going. But some workers got sick. Others were hurt, or died. Many of them were buried nearby.

We remember them.

Reflection Prompt:

Why do you think it's important to remember people who helped build something, even if we don't know all their names?

____

____

____

____

____

安息
木
Rest In
Peace

Put It In Order!

Activity Prompt:

Can you figure out the right order of how the workers built the Summit Tunnel?

Read all the steps below. Then write the numbers **1–8** in the boxes to show what happened first...and what came last!

☐ Workers set up wooden camps to live and eat in.

☐ Workers traveled across the ocean from China to California.

☐ They worked around the clock—through freezing storms, avalanches, and tough conditions.

☐ They climbed high into the snowy Sierra Nevada mountains.

☐ After three long years, the Summit Tunnel was finished!

☐ Explosives were packed into holes and set off to blast through the rock.

☐ They used hand tools to chip into the granite rock.

☐ After each explosion, workers cleared rubble and started again.

Design a Memorial

Activity Prompt:

Imagine a special way to honor the Chinese railroad workers who lost their lives. Draw a memorial here that shows what they meant to the United States.

The Golden Spike

Invisible No More

Photographers came to take pictures at the Golden Spike Ceremony—but they didn't take pictures of us. None of the Chinese workers who built the hardest parts of the railroad were included in the celebration. It was like we were not there.

But we were. We worked through snow and stone. We blasted tunnels and built tracks.

We were part of history, even if we were left out of the pictures.

It's an honor to tell you our story now, so the people who built this railroad are finally remembered.

Reflection Prompt:

Have you ever seen someone get left out, even when they helped?

What can we do to make sure everyone gets credit for their hard work?

Make a Memory Medal

Activity Prompt:

Not everyone who helped build the railroad got the credit they deserved. Some workers were left out of the photos and forgotten in the history books. Let's change that!

Create a special Memory Medal to honor someone from the story—like Wei, his uncle, or any of the Chinese workers who made a difference.

Instructions

- In the circle on the opposite page, draw and design a medal.
- Add words or pictures that show why your hero deserves to be remembered.
- You can decorate it with symbols of strength, teamwork, or courage!

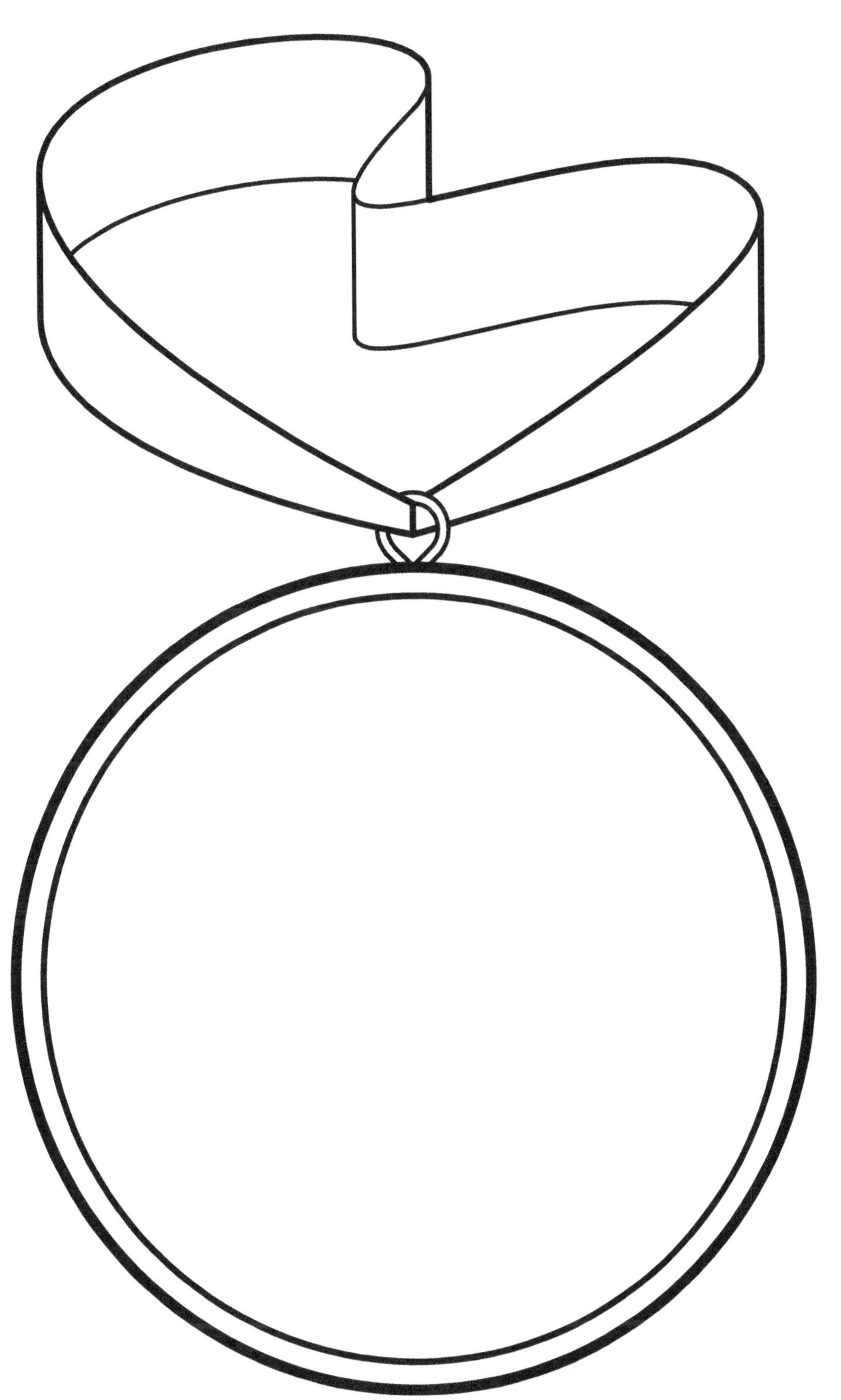

What Was the Chinese Exclusion Act?

Even after building one of the most important parts of America's railroad system, Chinese workers like me were still treated unfairly. In 1882, the U.S. passed a law called the Chinese Exclusion Act.

This law banned Chinese laborers from immigrating to the United States and made life harder for those already here.

Why did they do this? Because some people in power didn't want Chinese immigrants in the country.

They were afraid of people who looked, spoke, or lived differently than they did.

The same workers who helped build the country were now being shut out and forgotten.

When the Chinese Exclusion Act became a law, many people in the U.S. celebrated. Newspapers cheered. Some leaders said it was a victory. But those celebrations were based on racism and fear. The law hurt thousands of families and told people like us that we didn't belong.

It was the first law in U.S. history made to keep people out just because of where they came from. And it lasted from 1882 until 1943—more than 60 years!

That's why it matters to tell these stories now.

When we remember what Chinese workers did, and how they were treated, we can all do our part to try to make sure it never happens again.

HIP! HURRAH!
CHINESE EXLUDED
— The —
Democratic Chinese Exclusion Bill
has been signed

Remembering Today

In 2014, the U.S. government finally honored the Chinese railroad laborers. They were added to the Department of Labor's Hall of Honor.

And in 2024, Summit Camp, the place where many of us worked, and where some lost their lives building the tunnel, became a National Historic Landmark.

These honors came many years later. But they remind us that it's never too late to recognize courage and tell the truth.

When we pass these stories on, we make sure the people who built this country are remembered with the respect they deserve.

It's never too late to honor courage, teamwork, and truth.

Reflection Prompt:

Have you ever seen someone get left out, even when they helped? What can we do to make sure everyone gets credit for their hard work?

____

____

____

____

____

MIGRANT PRIDE
Celebrating Asian-American History

What We Carry Forward

So that's the story of how I did my part to build the most dangerous section of the Transcontinental Railroad when I was young.

We faced snowstorms, dangerous blasting powder, unfair pay, peril, starvation, and being left out. But we kept going together.

We showed courage. We showed teamwork. And we deserve to be remembered.

I am proud to represent the Chinese immigrants that made this tunnel happen.

There are very few written records about the Chinese workers like us who built the tunnels and tracks. Many Chinese American families keep our stories alive through **oral history**—sharing memories by word of mouth from grandparents to parents to kids.

Reflection Prompt:

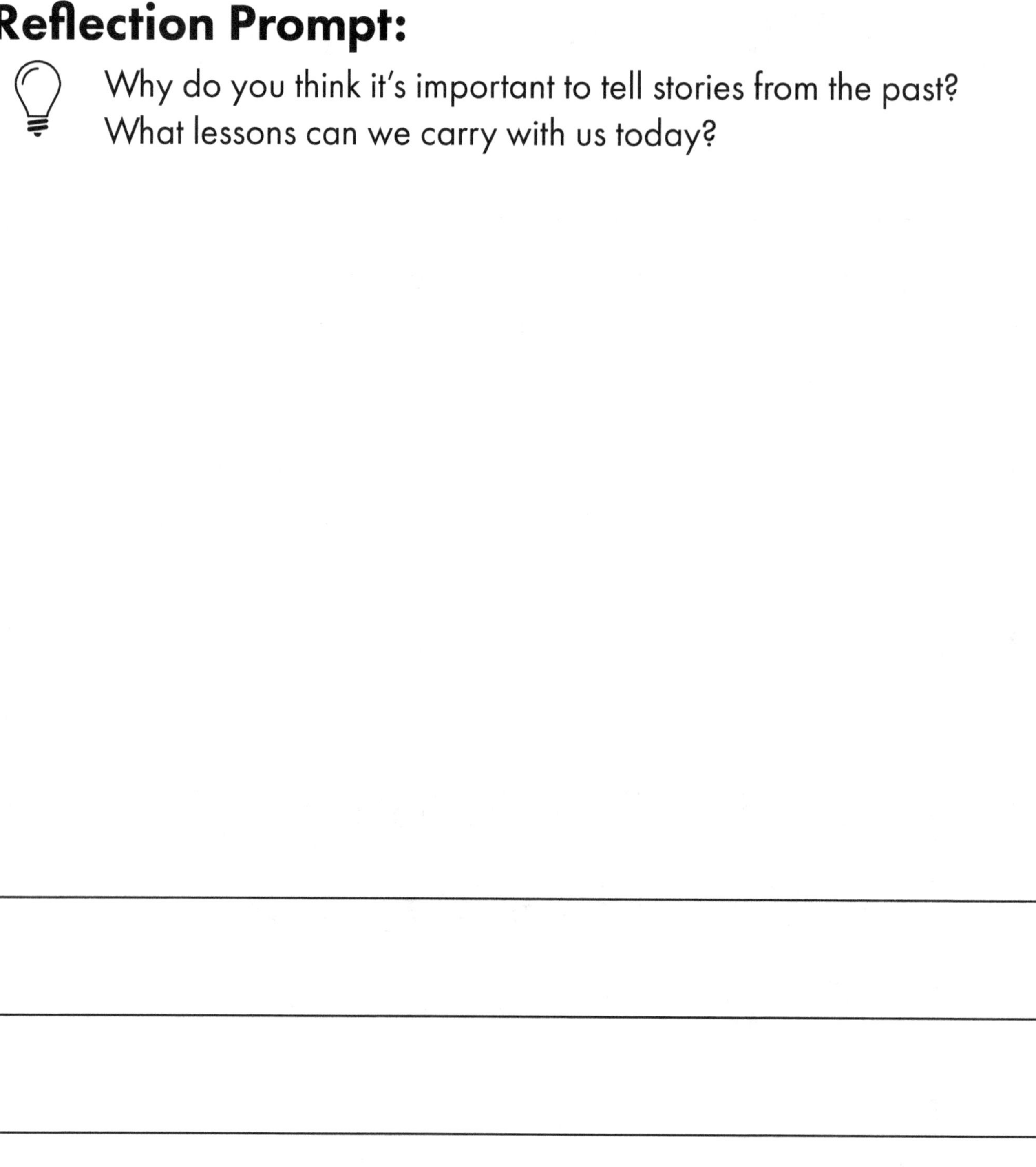

Why do you think it's important to tell stories from the past? What lessons can we carry with us today?

口述
And now, by
reading this book,
you are helping keep
that history alive.

Railroad Word Search!

Activity Prompt:

Can you find the words that tell the story of the Summit Tunnel? Each one is a piece of the history you just read about!

Use the word list to find the hidden words in the puzzle. *You can check your work on the answer key on Page 112.*

Reflection Prompt:

Pick one word from the Word Search on page 101. What does it make you think or feel? Why do you think this word matters to the story of the Summit Tunnel?

____

____

____

____

____

Every word tells a part of our story!

Timeline of the Railroad

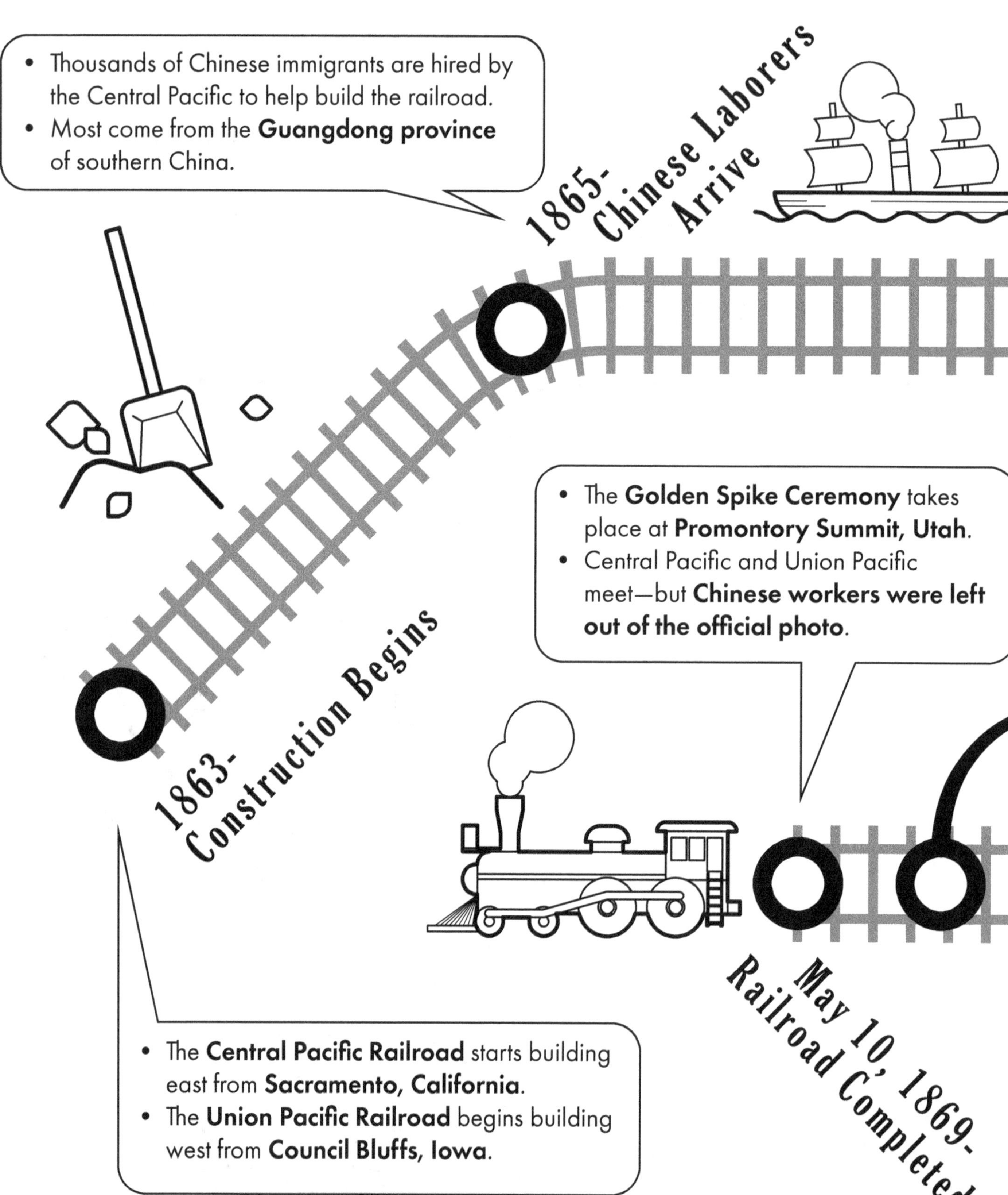

Chinese laborers start digging through solid granite in the **Sierra Nevada mountains**.
It's the **hardest** section of the entire railroad.

1866- Work Begins on Tunnel No. 6

Workers face snowstorms, avalanches, and explosions using **black powder** and **nitroglycerin**.
Chinese workers go on **strike** to demand fair pay and better hours.

1867 - Dangerous Progress

April 28, 1869 - A Record Day

Chinese crews lay **10 miles of track in a single day**—a world record that still holds today.

About This Story

Wei Zhang is a composite character inspired by the real experiences of Chinese laborers who helped build the **Summit Tunnel** and other parts of the **Transcontinental Railroad**.

While his name and story are imagined, the events he describes are based on historical records, oral histories, and expert research. There are very few written records about the individual Chinese workers who built the railroad—so we created Wei to honor the many people whose stories were left out of history books.

Wong Fook, Lee Chao, and Ging Cui with a parade float in Ogden, Utah, during a 1919 parade to celebrate the 50th anniversary of the completion of the Transcontinental Railroad. Image courtesy of Amon Carter Museum of American Art Archives.

If you or your family have stories or information to share about this history, we would love to hear from you.
Contact us at **hi@historicons.com**.

Honorary Historicon!

Certificate of Completion

This certifies that

has completed the journey through the Summit Tunnel and helped remember the Chinese workers who built American history.

张伟 *Wei Zhang*

Wei Zhang, Historicons Guide

Check Your Work!

Follow the Tracks:

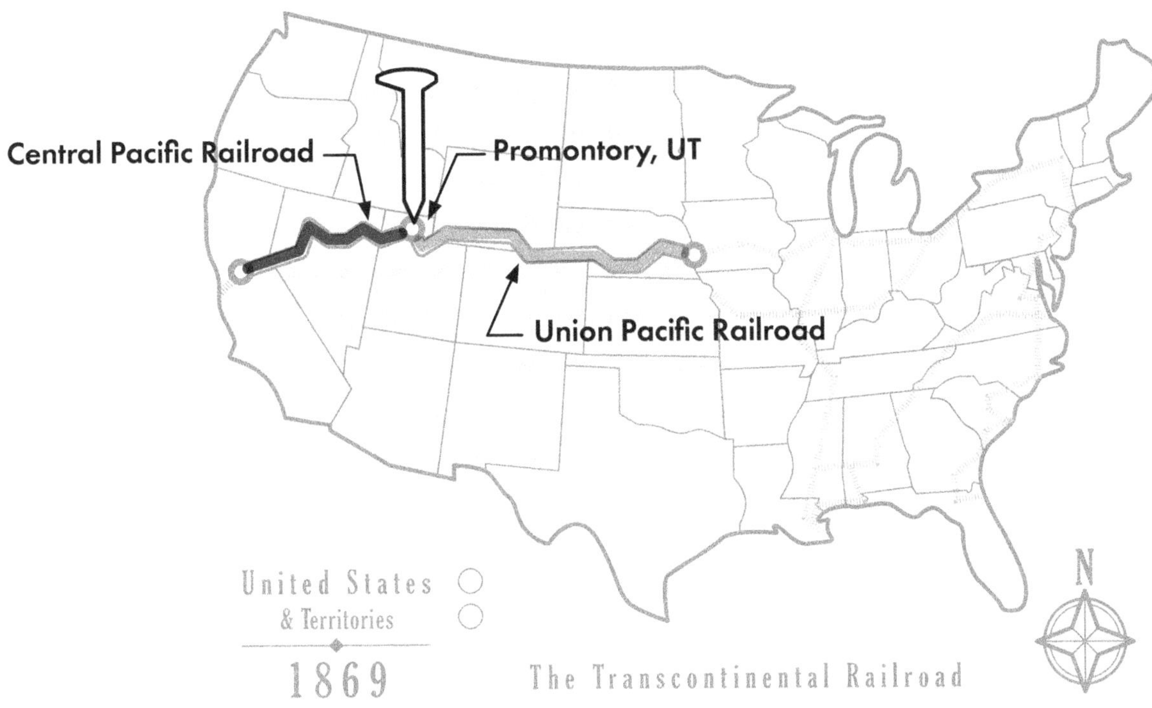

Tools of the Tunnel:

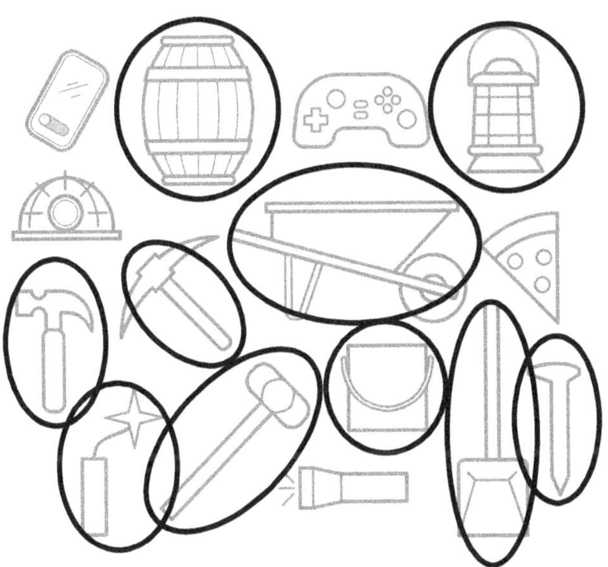

Put It In Order:

3 Workers set up wooden camps to live and eat in.

1 Workers traveled across the ocean from China to California.

7 They worked around the clock—through freezing storms, avalanches, and tough conditions.

2 They climbed high into the snowy Sierra Nevada mountains.

4 After three long years, the Summit Tunnel was finished!

5 Explosives were packed into holes and set off to blast through the rock.

6 They used hand tools to chip into the granite rock.

8 After each explosion, workers cleared rubble and started again.

Check Your Work (cont.)

Snow Tunnel Maze:

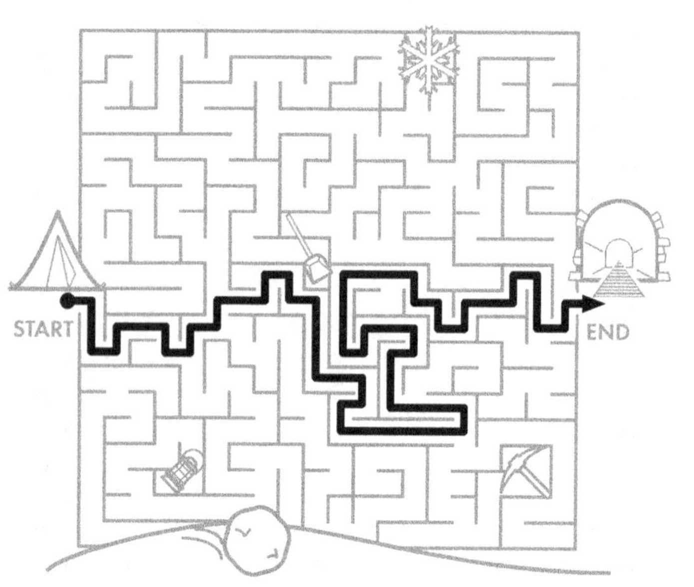

Railroad Word Search:

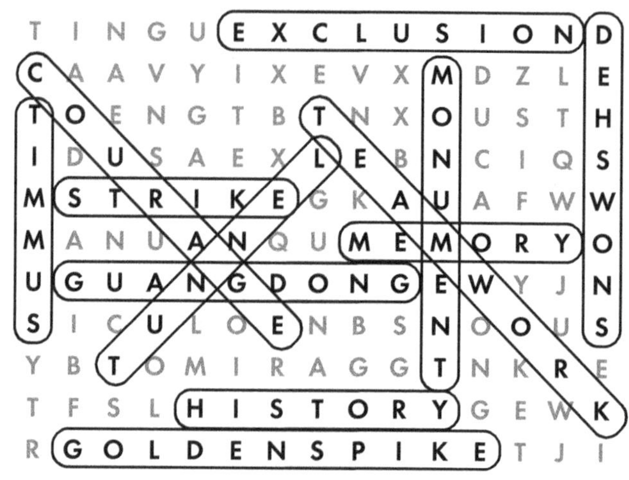

Parent/Educator Companian Resource

This guide includes:

- Strategies for Fostering Age-Appropriate Discussions on Diversity & Identity
- Discussion Guide
- Allies in Action
- Integrating Historicons in the Classroom
- Glossary
- Grade 3, 4, and 5 Lesson Plans
- More Resources

Strategies for Fostering Age-Appropriate Discussions on Diversity and Identity

When working with Historicons products, it's important to recognize the age and developmental differences among kids and adjust your conversations accordingly. Discussion about diversity, identity, and justice can feel daunting—but with a few simple strategies, you'll always **SCORE!**

S — **Start with the Basics**: Focus on simple concepts like fairness, respect, and uniqueness. Use honest, age-appropriate language and connect to kids' daily lives.

C — **Concrete Examples**: Talk about different family structures, languages spoken at home, or food traditions. This builds understanding and shows that difference is normal—and valuable.

O — **Open-Ended Questions**: Ask things like "What makes you feel special?" or "What's something kind someone has done for you?" to spark empathy and reflection.

R — **Root Conversations in Joy, Pride, and Positive Change**: Balance tough history with moments of resistance, celebration, and resilience. Spotlight heroes, not just hardships.

E — **Encourage Questions**: Let kids know it's okay to be curious— as long as we ask questions kindly. Creating space for questions promotes empathy and lifelong learning.

No two kids or classrooms are the same. Flexibility, curiosity, and care will help you create meaningful conversations that stick with your learners.

Discussion Guide

Use the built-in reflection prompts throughout the story as springboards for deeper conversations. Here are tips to help facilitate rich discussion:

Before Reading:

- What do you already know about trains or tunnels?

During Reading:

- Why do you think Wei and his uncle left China?

- What does it mean to speak up or take action for fairness, like in the strike?

After Reading:

- How do you think it felt to be left out of the "Golden Spike" photo?

- What can we do today to honor workers who didn't get credit?

Encourage kids to reflect in words, pictures, or actions. There's no one "right" answer. Every insight helps grow their empathy and understanding.

Allies in Action

Bringing History into Today

This section helps kids and families connect the Summit Tunnel story to real life today.

Learn More Together

Research the history of Chinese Americans in your own state or city. Are there local landmarks, museums, or people making change?

Support Asian American and Pacific Islander (AAPI) Communities

Explore local events for **AAPI Heritage Month (May)**. Visit an Asian-owned bookstore, eat at a Chinese restaurant, or support local artists.

Speak Up About Fairness

Have conversations about fairness at home or in school. Practice speaking up when someone is excluded or treated unfairly.

Keep Asking Questions

Learning history is about curiosity. If something in the story surprised you, follow it! Look it up. Ask more questions.

Take Action

Write a thank-you letter to a community elder, activist, or teacher who's helping keep history alive.

Integrating Historicons in the Classroom: Empowering Learning Through Diverse Narratives

Historicons' engaging puzzle-based games are designed to bring history to life in a captivating and inclusive manner. Educators and child development experts have collaborated to create a resource that not only imparts historical knowledge but also fosters empathy, critical thinking, and positive identity development. The versatility of Historicons makes it an invaluable addition to classroom instruction, spanning various subjects and grade levels. Here are some simple, powerful ways to use Historicons in your homeschooling or classroom:

Cultural Heritage Connections

Use the *Summit Tunnel* book during **AAPI Heritage Month (May)** to explore Chinese American history in a developmentally appropriate way.

Language Arts

- Retell the story using sequence words (first, then, finally).
- Pair with books like Coolies by Yin or The Year of the Boar and Jackie Robinson by Bette Bao Lord.
- Write from another character's perspective.

Social Studies

- Connect to units on westward expansion, immigration, or labor.
- Use the built-in timeline to explore primary sources and map skills.

- Talk about who is (and isn't) included in official stories. If something in the story surprised you, follow it! Look it up. Ask more questions.

SEL (Social-Emotional Learning)

- Reflect on Wei's courage and teamwork.
- Practice empathy by imagining how different characters felt.
- Discuss how we honor people whose names history left out.

Glossary

Avalanche — A sudden and fast-moving fall of snow, ice, and rocks down a mountain.

Black Powder — An early kind of explosive made from chemicals. Workers used it to blast through rock when building tunnels, but it was very dangerous.

Chinese Exclusion Act — A law passed in 1882 that unfairly stopped Chinese laborers from moving to the United States, just because of where they were from.

Displacement — When people are forced to leave their homes, land, or way of life—often because of unfair treatment.

Golden Spike — The special final nail hammered in to mark the completion of the Transcontinental Railroad in 1869.

Immigrant — A person who moves to a new country to live, work, or build a better life.

Indigenous — The first people to live on a land, like Native American communities in the U.S.

Laborer — A person who does hard physical work, often using their hands, strength, and skill.

Legacy

What someone leaves behind or is remembered for, like the impact of their actions or work.

Nitroglycerin

A powerful liquid explosive used to break tough rock. It was very unstable and could explode if shaken or moved too roughly.

Oral History

Stories and memories that are shared by talking, often passed down from older generations to younger ones.

Railroad Foreman

A person who is in charge of a group of workers and tells them what to do on a job like building train tracks or tunnels.

Strike

When workers refuse to do their jobs until they are treated more fairly.

Transcontinental Railroad

A train route that connected the East and West coasts of the U.S.—for the first time ever!

Tunnel

A long path carved through a mountain so trains could pass through it instead of going over.

More Resources:

Before diving into the Summit Tunnel activity book with your learners, take a few minutes to explore these tools:

1. Explore the History

Visit the 1882 Foundation's Summit Tunnel page to learn more about the true story. [https://1882foundation.org/programs/historic-preservation/summit-tunnel/]

2. Use the Glossary

Flip to page 121 anytime a student asks, *"What does that mean?"*

3. Review the Reflection Prompts

Preview the discussion questions from page 117 so you feel ready to talk about big ideas like fairness, courage, and exclusion.

4. Stay Curious

This book is just the beginning. Ask your kids or students what else they want to learn—and follow their lead!

Classroom Lesson Plans

This guide includes:

- Lesson plans for Grades 3-5
- Standards Alignment
- Materials required
- Detailed lesson activities
- Assessment of learning objectives

Lesson Plan: Grade 3

Lesson Title:

The Stories History Forgot

Students will be able to:

- Analyze the challenges and achievements of Chinese railroad workers.
- Understand how history is shaped by what's included and what's left out.
- Make personal connections between historical fairness and present-day inclusion.

Standards Alignment:

Common Core State Standards – ELA:

- **RI.3.3**: Describe the relationship between historical events.
- **W.3.1**: Write opinion pieces with supporting reasons.
- **SL.3.1**: Participate in collaborative discussions.

National Curriculum Standards for Social Studies (NCSS):

- **Theme 2**: Time, Continuity, and Change.
- **Theme 5**: Individual, Groups, and Institutions.

CASEL Social Emotional Learning Competency:

- **Social Awareness** – Empathize with others, including those from diverse backgrounds and cultures.

Learning for Justice (Social Justice Standards):

- **DI.3-5.6**: Understand that everyone deserves fair treatment.
- **JU.3-5.10**: Connect present injustices to historical roots.
- **HA.3-5.17**: Identify those who worked to create a fairer world.

Materials:

- Summit Tunnel book
- Page 64 (Mile 10) and Page 89 (Chinese Exclusion Act)
- Student journals or paper

Lesson Activities:

1. Timeline Mapping (15-20 mins)

Read Pages 5-9, 19-21, 31-39, 45-47, 64 and 89.

As as class, map events on a timeline:

- Wei's journey
- Tunnel No. 6 construction
- Mile 10 achievement
- Chinese Exclusion Act

Discuss: *What do these moments tell us about fairness and memory?*

2. Classroom Discussion (10 mins)

Prompt: *"If you were writing a history book, who would you include that might be left out? Why?"*

Chart student responses about inclusion and representation.

3. Reflective Writing (15 mins)

Prompt: *"Why is it important to learn stories like Wei's? What does it teach us about fairness and teamwork?"*

Encourage use of words like legacy, courage, equity, or inclusion.

Optional Extension:

Introduce the glossary word **immigrant**. Ask:

- *What is it like to move to a new place?*
- *What would you want people in your new community to know about you?*

Assessment:

- Student contributions during timeline and discussion.
- Reflection writing that demonstrates understanding of fairness and historical memory.

Lesson Plan: Grade 4

Lesson Title:

History Below the Surface

Students will be able to:

- Examine untold stories of Chinese railroad workers and their impact.
- Reflect on labor conditions and systemic unfairness.
- Recognize connections between exclusion in the past and today.

Standards Alignment:

Common Core State Standards – ELA:

- **RI.4.3**: Explain historical events, including cause/effect.
- **W.4.3**: Write narratives that describe real or imagined experiences.
- **SL.4.1**: Engage in discussions, building on others' ideas.

National Curriculum Standards for Social Studies (NCSS):

- **Theme 4**: Individual Development and Identity.
- **Theme 6**: Power, Authority, and Governance.

CASEL Social Emotional Learning Competency:

- **Responsible Decision Making** – Consider the ethical impact of decisions and understand consequences.

Learning for Justice (Social Justice Standards):

- **JU.3-5.10**: Understand how current treatment connects to the past.
- **HA.3-5.17**: Explain how people have stood up to injustice.

Materials:

- *Summit Tunnel* book
- Page 80 (Invisible No More) and 89 (Exclusion Act)
- Chart paper or whiteboard
- Drawing materials

Lesson Activities:

1. Read Aloud & Discussion (15 mins)

Read key pages 5-9, 19-21, 31-39, 80-81 and 89-91.

As a class, discuss:

- Why were Chinese workers left out of the photos?
- What was unfair about the Chinese Exclusion Act?
- What's changed, and what hasn't?

2. Timeline + Map Activity (15 mins)

- Add key events to a classroom timeline.
- Use Page 97 (What We Carry Forward) to reflect on legacy.
- Use the map activity (Pages 27-29) to visually reinforce the journey and meeting point in Promontory.

3. Creative Choice (20 mins)

Students choose to either:

1. Write a letter to Wei about why they think his story matters today, or
2. Design a new "history book page" that includes Wei and his crew.

Optional Extension:

Invite students to research or interview someone in their own family or community who immigrated to the United States.

Ask:

- What brought them here?
- What challenges did they face?
- How were they welcomed, or not?

Assessment:

- Participation in discussion.
- Depth of reflection in written or visual activity.

Lesson Plan: Grade 5

Lesson Title:

Whose Story Gets Told?

Students will be able to:

- Critically analyze how Chinese laborers were excluded from mainstream history.
- Explore structural injustices (wages, working conditions, exclusion laws).
- Make connections between historical remembrance and present-day advocacy.

Standards Alignment:

Common Core State Standards – ELA:

- **RI.5.3**: Explain relationships among people, events, and ideas.
- **SL.5.1**: Engage effectively in a range of collaborative discussions.
- **W.5.1**: Write opinion pieces on topics or texts.

National Curriculum Standards for Social Studies (NCSS):

- **Theme 6**: Power, Authority, and Governance.
- **Theme 10**: Civic Ideals and Practices.

CASEL Social Emotional Learning Competency:

- **Social Awareness** – Empathize with people from diverse backgrounds and recognize injustice.
- **Responsible Decision-Making** – Consider the ethical impact of decisions and understand consequences.

Learning for Justice (Social Justice Standards):

- **JU.3-5.10**: Understand how current treatment connects to the past.
- **HA.3-5.17**: Explain how people have stood up to injustice.

Materials:

- *Summit Tunnel* book
- Printed copies of Pages 67-69 (The Summer We Spoke Up), 89-91 (Exclusion Act) and 93-95 (Remembering Today)
- Chart paper or whiteboard
- Writing journals or lined paper

Lesson Activities:

1. Cause & Effect Analysis (20 mins)

Read key pages 5-9, 19-21, 31-39, 80-81 and 89-91.

Break into groups to analyze:

- What led to unfair treatment?
- What were the effects?
- What can we learn from this?

Have groups share their key takeaways to the class.

2. Modern Connections (15 mins)

As a class, explore a current example of exclusion or underrepresentation (such as underrepresentation in books, sports, politics, or STEM careers). The teacher can share a few examples or articles to guide the discussion.

Sample Discussion Starters:

- What group is being left out or treated unfairly?
- How is this similar to the story of the Chinese railroad workers?
- What progress has society made since the Chinese railroad workers built the Summit Tunnel? What still needs to change?

Suggested examples to explore::

- Women in science or engineering
- Disability access in schools
- LGBTQ+ participation in sports
- Native American land rights
- Asian American representation in film

3. Opinion Essay (20 mins)

Prompt: "Why is it important to learn the stories of the Chinese railroad workers? What can this history teach us about fairness and courage today?"

Encourage citing details from the text.

Optional Extension:

Show students two textbook pages or online articles about the Transcontinental Railroad.
Then ask:

- Are Chinese railroad workers mentioned?

- Are Native communities mentioned?
- What's missing?

Have students write a letter to a textbook editor or website saying what should be added or updated, and why it matters.

Assessment:

- Group cause/effect analysis.
- Opinion essay with clear evidence and argument.
- Ability to draw connections to present-day issues.

About 1882 Foundation

Since our founding as *The 1882 Project*, we have sought to promote public awareness of the history and continuing significance of the Chinese Exclusion Laws. These laws were first enacted in the year 1882. They prohibited Chinese from immigrating to the United States and barred them from citizenship. In 1943, during World War II, Congress rescinded the laws for political and military reasons. Until that time, there had been no acknowledgment of six decades of federally sanctioned violations of civil rights, racial discrimination, or violent attacks over generations on Chinese and other Asians in America.

In 2011-2012, we were successful in our efforts to have Congress "express regret" for the exclusion laws and reaffirming that the nation is founded upon the principle "that all persons are created equal." The 1882 Project Foundation*, as we are officially known, continues to broaden public understanding of the laws, their history, and their relevance today through its educational programs and initiatives that include supporting projects that preserve and interpret the history of Chinese and Asians in America about their contributions to the United States.

*The 1882 Project Foundation is an IRS-approved 501(c)(3) organization formed in the state of Virginia. All donations are tax deductible.

Descendants of Chinese Transcontinental Railroad workers and other members of the Chinese American community gather for a photo on the 150th anniversary of the railroad's completion at Golden Spike National Historical Park in Promontory, Utah, U.S. May 10, 2019. Photo by Corky Lee.

The 1882 Foundation is proud to partner with Historicons in producing this first-of-its-kind Coloring + Activity Book about Chinese workers on the Transcontinental Railroad. This partnership represents for us another step in engaging young people about the history of Chinese in America and in how we can expand understanding of the Asian American experience through storytelling.

Learn more about us and support our mission at **www.1882foundation.org.**

About Historicons®

At Historicons, we believe history should

We create activity books, puzzles, and classroom materials that bring true, untold stories to life—especially the ones too often left out of textbooks. Our products help kids connect to the past in creative, meaningful ways, so they grow up informed, empathetic, and proud of their story.

Each Historicons product is designed to:

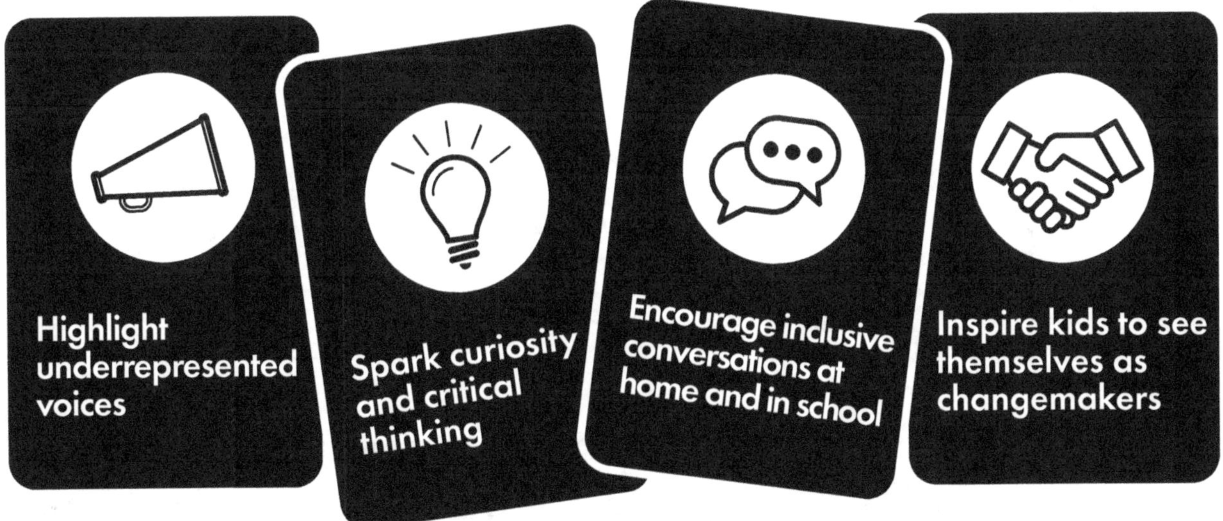

Whether it's learning about Chinese railroad workers, disability activists, or LGBTQ+ trailblazers, every Historicons story helps kids ask big questions, build empathy, and honor those who made a difference.

Discover more at **www.historicons.com**.

Explore other screen-free, story-powered learning tools from Historicons!

At Historicons, we create puzzle games, activity books, and classroom materials that bring real history to life. Each product is designed by educators and child development experts to help kids learn through creativity, curiosity, and inclusive storytelling.

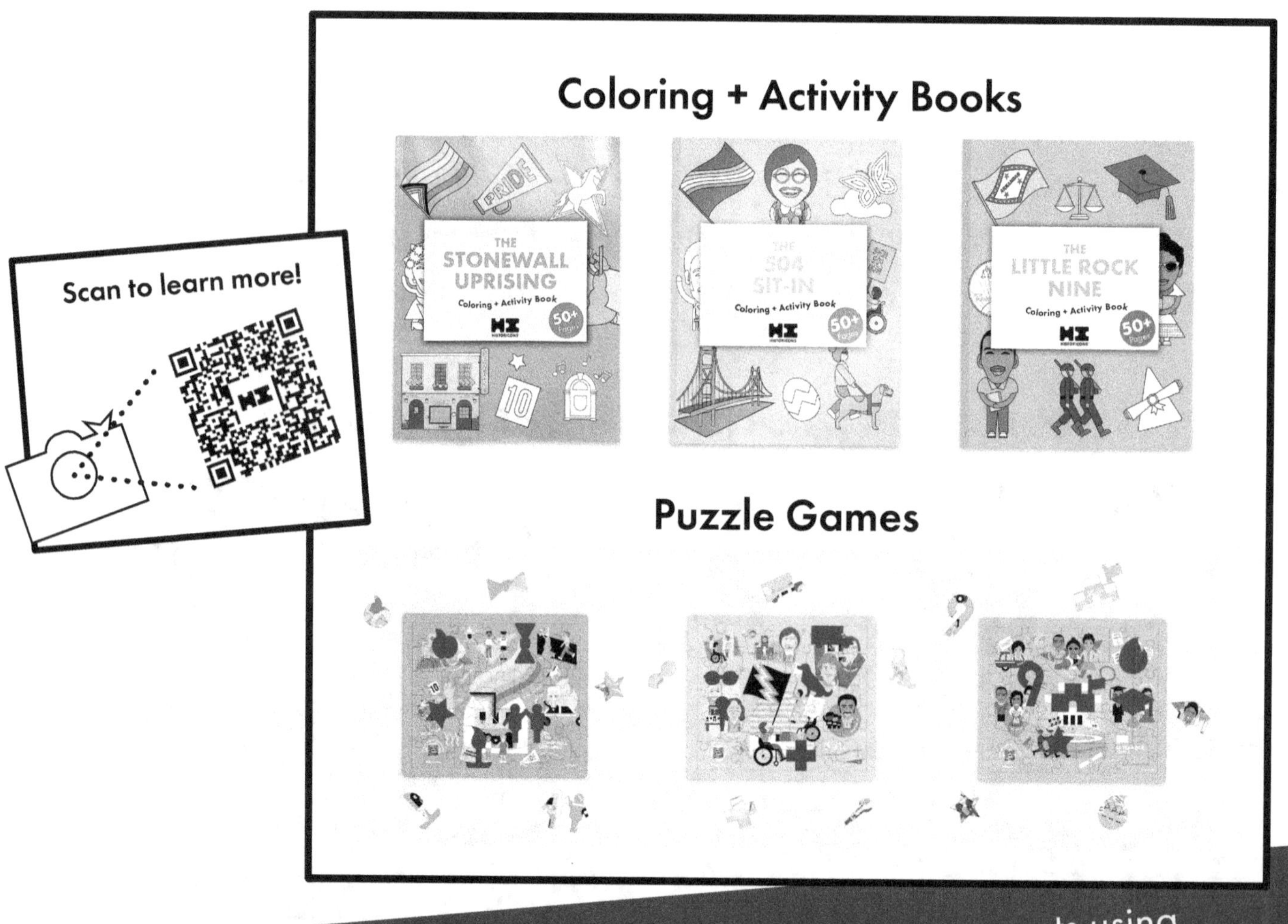

www.ingramcontent.com/pod-product-compliance
Lightning Source LLC
Chambersburg PA
CBHW080740120726
48001CB00009B/2640